how2become

KS3 ENGLISH IS EASY

(SPOKEN ENGLISH)

THE
REVISION
SERIES

www.How2Become.com

As part of this product you have also received FREE access to online tests that will help you to pass Key Stage 3 ENGLISH
(Spoken English).

To gain access, simply go to:

www.PsychometricTestsOnline.co.uk

Get more products
for passing any test at:

www.How2Become.com

Orders: Please contact How2Become Ltd, Suite 14, 50 Churchill Square Business Centre, Kings Hill, Kent ME19 4YU.

You can order through Amazon.co.uk under ISBN 9781911259039, via the website www.How2Become.com or through Gardners.com.

ISBN: 9781911259039

First published in 2016 by How2Become Ltd.

Typeset for How2Become Ltd by Anton Pshinka.

Disclaimer

Every effort has been made to ensure that the information contained within this guide is accurate at the time of publication. How2Become Ltd is not responsible for anyone failing any part of any selection process as a result of the information contained within this guide. How2Become Ltd and their authors cannot accept any responsibility for any errors or omissions within this guide, however caused. No responsibility for loss or damage occasioned by any person acting, or refraining from action, as a result of the material in this publication can be accepted by How2Become Ltd.

The information within this guide does not represent the views of any third party service or organisation.

CONTENTS

THE
REVISION
SERIES

UNDERSTANDING THE CURRICULUM

THE NATIONAL CURRICULUM

State-funded schools are governed by a set curriculum of 'core' subjects which must form part of children's timetables. These core subjects are essential for providing key knowledge and skills, which will help us to produce well-rounded and educated citizens.

In Key Stage 3 (ages 11-14), the core subjects that must be taught in schools include the following:

- **English**
- **Maths**
- **Science**
- **Art and Design**
- **Citizenship**
- **Computing**
- **Design and Technology**
- **Languages**
- **Geography**
- **History**
- **Music**
- **Physical Education**

All schools, Key Stage 1 to Key Stage 4, must also teach Religious Studies to their students, and children will have Sex Education classes from the age of 11. However, parents are given the option of pulling their children out from these subjects.

THE IMPORTANCE OF ENGLISH

Students are taught the importance of English via spoken language, reading, writing and vocabulary. Not only is this a core subject which all students are required to undertake, but this subject is an integral part of other school subjects. Children will need to have a strong grasp of the English Language, which will prove vital if they are to be successful across their school subjects.

The fundamental aims of the English subject include:

- Reading with fluency and ease;

- Demonstrating a good understanding of the English Language;

- Highlighting the importance of reading, and allowing students to read for both pleasure and academia;

- Appreciating the English Language and its heritage;

- Acquiring a strong English vocabulary to improve students' knowledge in regards to reading, writing and listening;

- Writing strong literature; and adapting their writing and language in order to demonstrate its purpose, context and audience;

- Improving children's confidence in their English abilities, allowing them to become competent in the English Language via verbal and written communication.

In Key Stage 3, the English subject focuses on four main 'disciplines':

- **Reading;**
- **Writing;**
- **Grammar and Vocabulary;**
- **Spoken English.**

The aforementioned disciplines are all used to teach students vital skills for both academia and the outside world.

READING AND WRITING

Reading and writing form the very basic skills that every person should obtain from an early age.

The skill of reading is invaluable for students, since it allows them to read for pleasure as well as for information. The ability to read is also necessary across other school subjects and therefore it is imperative that students are able to read fluently and effectively.

Writing is a great skill which can be altered to reflect different contexts, purposes and audiences. In Key Stage 3, students are required to write different literary texts for different purposes. Thus, this requires a strong level of knowledge regarding vocabulary and grammar.

GRAMMAR AND VOCABULARY

Students in Key Stage 3 will need to extend knowledge which was obtained in Key Stage 2.

Teachers will need to enhance students' knowledge by teaching them the importance of grammar, punctuation and spelling. These key areas allow students to not only analyse literary texts, but also improve their own writing style.

Linguistically, students will need to develop a strong understanding of English terminology, and learn how this can be applied to literary texts. This includes learning the ability to use appropriate vocabulary, understanding the meaning of words and phrases, and learning how to analyse, practise and apply literary techniques in their own work.

SPOKEN ENGLISH

Not only is written communication an important aspect of the English Language, but the ability to speak fluent English is just as vital.

Spoken English is used every day, in a range of different contexts. Developing a person's speaking skills will allow for well-rounded citizens who have the ability to communicate effectively.

Speaking skills allow students to become more confident at speaking out loud, and to engage with the English Language competently.

Having a strong understanding of the English Language will allow students to become fluent in written and spoken English. This will allow them to communicate effectively with the world around them, thus allowing children to become engaged in cultural, social and economic debates, as well as intellectual debates.

ENGLISH SUBJECT CONTENT

Below we have broken down the aims and objectives of each 'discipline' for the subject. This will hopefully give you some idea of what will be assessed, and how you can improve different areas in your reading, writing and speaking abilities.

READING

Pupils will be taught how to:

❏ Develop an appreciation of the English language.
❏ Engage with a variety of literary texts including:
- *Non-fiction, fiction, plays and poetry. Texts that cover a wide range of genres, eras, authors, styles and narratives.*
- *Reading books for pleasure and academia.*
- *Understanding the importance of Shakespeare's works.*

❏ Engage with challenging texts by:
- *Learning new vocabulary, grammar and literary techniques.*
- *Analysing key words and phrases.*
- *Making inferences and assumptions based on the information provided.*
- *Knowing the meaning behind the text, including the purpose, audience and context.*

❏ Read critically:
- *Recognising different literary techniques.*
- *Analysing narration, characterisation, style, themes and genre.*
- *Comparing two or more texts (cross-examination).*
- *Understanding meaning through figurative language, word choices, structure and conventions.*

WRITING

Pupils will be taught how to:

❑ Write with fluency, ease and control.
❑ Write a range of different literary texts including:
- *Strong, persuasive, narrative essays.*
- *Short stories, plays and poetry.*
- *Imaginative writing.*
- *Formal letters.*
- *Scripts and presentations.*
❑ Plan, draft and proofread writing:
- *Plan and draft your ideas. Think about:*
  - *Characters, narrative, themes, motives, style, context, audience and purpose.*
- *Carefully choosing grammar and understanding the importance of vocabulary.*
- *Structuring your writing format in a clear and concise manner.*
- *Understanding the importance of audience, and how your writing can be influential.*
❑ Be original and creative.
❑ Use the English language in a way that is expressive, creative, informative, imaginative or personal.

SPOKEN ENGLISH

Pupils will be taught how to:

❑ Verbally communicate to a high standard by:
- *Speaking confidently, persuasively and effectively.*
❑ Improve their speaking skills by engaging with particular grammar and vocabulary:
- *Understanding what type of spoken English they should use and in what context.*
- *Understanding how to get their point across in the best possible way.*
❑ Participate in verbal debates, discussions and presentations.
❑ Improve speaking skills such as volume, tone, enthusiasm and interaction.

GRAMMAR AND VOCABULARY

Pupils will be taught how to:

☐ Improve pre-existing grammar and vocabulary skills taught in Key Stage 2.
☐ Understand the importance of grammar:
  ▪ *How this creates meaning.*
  ▪ *The impact this has on the audience.*
☐ Analyse key words and phrases:
  ▪ *Why they are used.*
  ▪ *The meaning behind them.*
  ▪ *What is the author implying/inferring?*
☐ Understand what grammar and vocabulary to use. Think about:
  ▪ *What kind of literary text they are writing/reading.*
  ▪ *What do words mean and how can they be interpreted?*
  ▪ *Is it a formal or informal piece of literary text?*

English is not only a core subject, but a topic that impacts upon every aspect of our daily lives. As you can see, it is imperative that students are able to engage with the English Language, in order to improve on vital skills and knowledge.

USING THIS GUIDE

This guide focuses specifically on Key Stage 3 English (Spoken English). This book will focus on the basics that every child will need to know, to ensure top marks across the English subject.

REMEMBER – It's really important that you have great communication skills.

HOW WILL I BE ASSESSED?

In Key Stage 3, children will be assessed based on Levels. These years do not count towards anything, and are simply a reflection of progression and development. The first years of secondary school are in place in order to determine whether or not pupils are meeting the minimum requirements, and are integral for preparing pupils for their GCSE courses.

Although these years do not count towards any final results, they do go a long way to deciphering which GCSEs you will pick up. For example, if you were excelling in Art and Design in KS3, you could consider taking this subject at GCSE. The subjects that you choose at GCSE will impact upon your future aspirations, including further education and career opportunities.

You will be monitored and assessed throughout these schooling years, via the following:

- Ongoing teacher assessments;
- Term progress reports;
- Summative assessments at the end of each academic year.

By the end of Key Stage 3, pupils are expected to achieve Levels 5 or 6.

THE
REVISION
SERIES

INCREASE YOUR CHANCES

Below is a list of GOLDEN NUGGETS that will help YOU and your CHILD to prepare for Key Stage 3 English.

Golden Nugget 1 – Read stuff out loud

You can improve your speaking by reading books and information out loud. Instead of reading it in your head, practise your English ability by reading out loud.

Pay attention to how quickly you speak, the tone of your voice, and your pronunciation.

Golden Nugget 2 – Get involved!

Get involved with social interactions. This will really help you to improve on your spoken English. Afterschool sporting teams, raising your hand in the classroom and talking to lots of people, are all great ways to improve your speaking ability.

Golden Nugget 3 – Listen to others

You will learn a lot by listening to the way other people speak. This will help with your own speaking abilities.

> ***TIP*** *– Listen to people or a tape recorder and then repeat the way in which they speak. This will help to better your pronunciation.*

Golden Nugget 4 – Improve your confidence

Practise communicating verbally, as well as in your writing. This will allow you to improve your confidence and English ability.

> ***TIP*** *– Have discussions and debates in order to gain confidence in public speaking.*
>
> ***TIP*** *–Deliver presentations to family members and friends. This will really help to improve your confidence.*

Golden Nugget 5 – Stay positive!

The most important piece of preparation advice for parents, is to make sure that your child is positive and relaxed about these tests.

Don't let assessments worry you, and certainly don't let them worry your child.

TIP – Make sure the home environment is as comfortable and relaxed as possible for your child.

Golden Nugget 6 – Communicate with different people

The more confidence you have, the better your spoken English will be. Talk to your friends and family, and work on your spoken English and pronunciation. If you find this relatively easy, why not talk to people you are not so familiar with? Maybe talk to someone at school you might not usually talk to. See how well you get on with communicating with them.

Golden Nugget 7 – Managing your nerves

It is important for anyone who wishes to improve their speaking skills, to be able to manage their nerves. Nerves show in a number of ways – sweating, stuttering, shaky body, lack of eye contact etc. Therefore it is important that you feel confident when speaking in public.

TIP – Practise in front of a mirror. This will help you to not only improve on your speaking skills, but it will also allow you to see what you look like when presenting/speaking.

Once you have some confidence, why not practise in front of people you feel comfortable with? This will really help you overcome any nerves.

Golden Nugget 8 – Check out our other revision resources

We have a range of other English resources to help you prepare for EVERY element of KS3 English.

THE
REVISION
SERIES

MANAGING NERVES

MANAGING NERVES

FEAR OF PUBLIC SPEAKING

Alongside their studies, students are also being assessed on their speaking abilities and how well they can communicate with other people.

Public speaking is a key component of the English subject, and students will be assessed in how well they can articulate themselves vocally.

It is common for speaking in public to be a fear for most people, adults included! From a young age, it is important that these skills are enhanced for future preparation. Ultimately, this will improve confidence.

SIGNS OF NERVES

Not everyone loves speaking out loud! Especially for young people, some people find it hard to find their voice.

Unless they're speaking to close friends or family, some people are really shy when it comes to talking in public.

Here are a few signs to look out for which suggest a person is nervous:

- Perspiration (sweating)
- Shaky body
- Trembling
- Fidgeting
- Lack of eye contact (looking at the floor)
- Breathlessness

MANAGING NERVES

RELAX!
Everyone can improve
their speaking skills!

HOW TO MANAGE YOUR NERVES

There are a few simple, but extremely effective tips to help you manage your nerves!

<u>When you are asked to speak in public, or if you wish to improve your speaking ability, consider the following and apply them to your speech:</u>

1. Practise using notes.
You can manage your nerves by knowing what you are going to be talking about. This will improve your memory, and give you some idea of what to talk about.
2. Practise using cue cards.
After you've practised using notes, try shortening these notes down and write them on simply que cards. This will allow you to quickly look down and read key-words or phrases, and thus trigger what you want to say.
3. Watch yourself in the mirror.
This is a great way to practise gestures, facial expressions and your approach to speaking. Stand tall and upright. Try to convey a calm, welcoming demeanour.
4. Don't speak too fast.
Many people who are asked to speak in public try to rush through what they have to say, in order to finish quicker. This is not a good idea. Try to pace yourself and take regular deep breaths.
5. Exercise.
Prior to speaking, you should exercise. This will ensure that your heart rate is raised, and your brain is active.
6. Practise with friends and family.
The best way to improve your performance is to simply practise. Sit down with your friends and family and practise speaking with them. This will undoubtedly increase confidence.

MANAGING NERVES

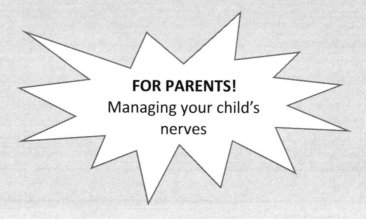

FOR PARENTS!
Managing your child's
nerves

Although gaining the confidence to speak fluently is primarily down to the child, there are a few things YOU can do to help your child improve their speech.

Encourage your child to persevere.

Focus on the positives.

Reward your child when they accomplish what they are trying to do.

Stay calm. Ensure their home environment is relaxed.

Communicate verbally with your child as much as you can.

Try a few relaxation techniques with your child. This will ensure that they feel more comfortable about speaking.

Reassure your child that it is okay not to be perfect.

Keep going. Don't let your child give up.

THE REVISION SERIES

WHY DO WE SPEAK DIFFERENTLY?

WHY DO WE SPEAK DIFFERENTLY?

UNDERSTANDING SPEECH

When we walk down the street, we will hear many people speaking English. But why does everyone sound different?

Well, there are a number of factors that change the way in which a person speaks. There are two key words that you need to know regarding spoken English: **idiolect** and **sociolect**.

- Idiolect is the way in which an individual talks. For example, you may talk differently from other members of your family.

- Sociolect is the speech used within a particular group. For example, the younger generation have a different social dialect compared to the older generation.

It is important that you have a good understanding about speech and why people sound different.

FACTORS THAT INFLUENCE LANGUAGE

There are many factors to take into consideration when asking why people speak differently.

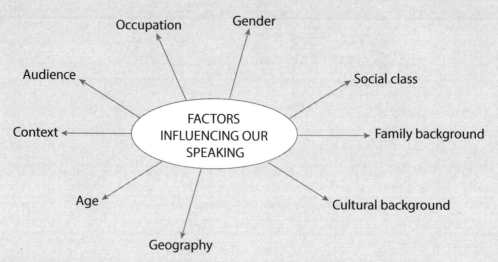

Can you work out how the above factors influence the way we speak?

WHY DO WE SPEAK DIFFERENTLY?

GEOGRAPHICAL INFLUENCES

- Depending on where people come from, depends on how they speak.

- Variations of the English language come from **regional dialects**. This is based on location and where each person is situated in terms of region (i.e. south, east, north and west).

- The term 'accent' is often related to where a person comes from. They sound different from people who live/come from somewhere else.

AGE INFLUENCES

- The way children are raised in today's society is very different to how their parents or grandparents might have been raised.

- Age is a key factor to consider with regards to language.

EDUCATIONAL INFLUENCES

- Every child will attend school. During which, they will learn from a range of people, from teachers to their peers.

- Education not only allows for pupils to be taught how to communicate, but their learning is constantly being influenced.

- The way in which people act and talk on the playground is very different to how people communicate in a classroom.

WHY DO WE SPEAK DIFFERENTLY?

FAMILY INFLUENCES

- This is a key factor. Everyone is raised differently, and therefore the way we speak is heavily influenced by our childhood.

- Parents and siblings are a key component in the way we learn.

- Language and habits are taught, as children pick up things that are said.

AUDIENCE INFLUENCES

- Who are you talking to?

- Depending on who you are talking to, will depend on how you speak.

- For example, are you talking to friends, parents, a teacher or a doctor?

SOCIAL CLASS INFLUENCES

- People from different social classes often speak differently.

- People from lower income families are expected to speak differently from people of a wealthier background.

WHY DO WE SPEAK DIFFERENTLY?

OCCUPATION INFLUENCES

- People from different jobs will use different language and address people in different ways.

- For example, jobs in law and medical professions will use very technical, wordy, professional language which highlights not only their expertise, but the **sociolect** which relates to that specific group of people.

GENDER INFLUENCES

- The way in which women and men speak can be compared.

- It is often said that men are more 'foul-mouthed' as opposed to women. However, this is not the case and is simply a stereotype.

OTHER INFLUENCES

- Are you speaking in a formal or informal context?

- Consider the purpose of your speech?

- Who are you addressing?

- Are you presenting a presentation or a speech? Are you rehearsing a play or a piece of poetry?

EXERCISES

EXERCISE 1

Identify your idiolect. Consider the following:

- **Expressions** – are there any expressions you use? How do you express yourself? Are you quite visual? I.e. do you use your hands?

- **Body language** – what does your body language say when you are speaking? How do you hold yourself in conversation?

- **Word choice** – what words do you say?

- **Style** – how do you normally speak to someone? Do you pause a lot? Do you ramble on? Are you able to keep a conversation going?

EXERCISE 2

Now analyse the way one of your parents or grandparents speak. Consider the same as you did for the above question:

- Expressions
- Body language
- Word choice
- Style

How does their language differ from your own? Why do you think this is?

EXERCISE 3

The younger generation use a variety of expressions and words that the older generation are less familiar with. Use the space below to write words and/or expressions, which show a difference in language between the younger and older generation.

WORD / EXPRESSION	DEFINITION

EXERCISE 4

For the following sentences / expressions, write down an alternative way to speak that sentence / expression. For each one, you will be given a factor of influence (social class, gender, occupation etc.) for which you must write a different way to write the same sentence.

<u>The first one has been done for you.</u>

a) Are you coming in for dinner?

SOCIAL CLASS

- Is one coming in for their supper?

b) Hello my friend, how are you?

AGE

_____

c) Ay up, wassa matter?

LOCATION

_____

EXERCISE 5

How do you think technology has impacted the way the younger generation speak compared to their grandparents? Use examples to support your answer.

_____
_____
_____
_____
_____
_____
_____

EXERCISE 6

For this exercise, you will need a friend, parent, grandparent or anyone you can think of.

The aim of this task is to write down key characteristics about the way in which the other person speaks, and then mimic one another. Practise speaking in the way that the other person does, to see how different your style of language differs.

Below I have created a spider diagram of the key things you should look out for when trying to imitate the other person.

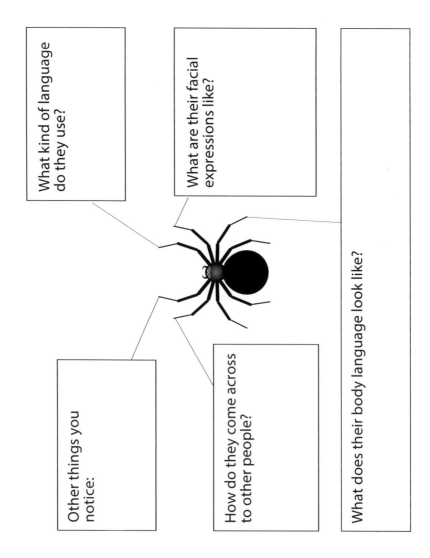

TOP TIPS

WHY DO WE SPEAK DIFFERENTLY?

- There are many factors to consider in regards to the English language and how we speak:

  o   Occupation

  o   Location

  o   Gender

  o   Social class

  o   Audience

  o   Family

  o   Education

  o   Context

  o   Age

- You should try and talk to different people, from a range of different backgrounds.

- Remember differ people have different **idiolects**.

- A **sociolect** is associated with a group of people who share the same language (i.e. medical professionals speak a very technical form of English language compared to people in other professions).

- Technology has had a huge impact on the way the younger generation speaks. Mobile phones, messaging software and other devices have led to short-hand for some words developing. Some people use the same language in their actual speech.

- Paying close attention to the way other people speak is a great way to understand the differences between how people communicate.

THE
REVISION
SERIES

FORMAL VS. INFORMAL SPEECH

FORMAL VS. INFORMAL

KNOWING WHEN TO USE FORMAL AND INFORMAL

In speech, you will be speaking for a very specific purpose and audience. Therefore, your speech needs to be tailored to cater for the people who are listening.

FORMAL LANGUAGE	INFORMAL LANGUAGE
Formal language should always be used on a professional level. This type of language is great for work-related/serious speeches, news reports and emails to employers.	Informal language should be used between friends and family. This is like a 'general chat' – language you often use in everyday context. Often uses colloquialism.
Things to consider: • Keep your writing clear, and to the point. • Avoid words such as "well", "nice", "you know" etc. • Avoid friendly chat words and phrases. • Use similes and metaphors. Figurative language is great at making your writing more powerful. • Your writing needs to be clearly structured. • Avoid contracted words. • Avoid slang terminology.	This would include diary entries, emails to friends/families, informal social gatherings etc. Things to consider: • Contracted words often sound more natural. This is acceptable in informal writing. • Even with informal language, never swear! • Don't waffle on. • Informal language is often written in the way that people talk.

EXERCISES

EXERCISE 1

For the following sentences, tick whether each sentence is written using formal or informal language.

SENTENCE	FORMAL	INFORMAL
Alright mate		
Yours faithfully		
Catch ya later!		
But, I don't want to…		
On the contrary…		
What up…		
Kind regards		

EXERCISE 2

Give an example of a time when you would need to speak formally. Why would you need to speak formally in this situation as opposed to informally?

_____

_____

_____

Give an example of a time when you would need to speak informally. Why would you need to speak informally in this situation as opposed to formally?

_____

_____

_____

EXERCISE 3

Draft an email to the head teacher. Your email should be written using formal language.

EXERCISE 4

Using your answer to Exercise 3, change the language used in the email to informal language.

_____

_____

_____

_____

_____

_____

_____

_____

_____

_____

_____

EXERCISE 5

Write a formal speech about whether or not Religious Education should be taught in schools.

_____

_____

_____

_____

_____

_____

_____

_____

_____

_____

_____

_____

_____

_____

_____

_____

_____

_____

EXERCISE 6

Now, using the same topic, re-write your work, using informal language.

_____

_____

_____

_____

_____

_____

_____

_____

_____

_____

_____

_____

_____

_____

_____

_____

_____

_____

_____

_____

_____

EXERCISE 7

Below are sentences that are written in an informal way. Circle the informal word/s in each sentence and then re-write the sentence using formal language.

a) My mum and I spent the whole day together.

_____

b) The teacher said I had to say sorry.

_____

c) I ain't going to tell you.

_____

d) The cops arrested a crook for theft.

_____

e) She caught on to what we were planning.

_____

f) I was told I had to get better at my reading.

_____

g) I had a free crib tonight, because my parents had gone on holiday.

_____

h) I'm broke. I have no moolah to go out at the weekend.

_____

i) Cheers. You're the shiz!

_____

FORMAL VS. INFORMAL

- It is important that you understand the difference between formal language and informal language. Not only that, but it is also important to know when to use each one.

- Here is the answer for exercise 1:

SENTENCE	FORMAL	INFORMAL
Alright mate		✓
Yours faithfully	✓	
Catch ya later!		✓
But, I don't want to…		✓
On the contrary…	✓	
What up…		✓
Kind regards	✓	

- Here are the answers for exercise 7:

a) Mum

   My mother and I spent the whole day together.

b) Say sorry

   The teacher said I had to apologise.

c) Ain't

   I am not going to tell you.

d) Cops / crook

   The police arrested a criminal for theft.

e) Caught on

   She figured out what we were planning.

f) Get better

I was told I had to improve my reading.

g) Crib

I had a free house tonight because my parents had gone on holiday.

h) Broke / moolah

I'm poor. I have no money to go out at the weekend.

i) Cheers / shiz

Thank you. You are the best!

- Practise using different forms of informal and formal language.

- Understand when to use each one.

- It's a good idea to write down what you want to say, and think of ways of how this would be perceived to the audience.

- Remember, presentations, structured debates, formal speeches and any situation that requires seriousness or professionalism will require you to use formal language.

- Situations that occur between friends and family will use informal language.

THE
REVISION
SERIES

HOW TO IMPROVE YOUR SPOKEN ENGLISH

HOW TO IMPROVE YOUR SPOKEN ENGLISH

As part of the national curriculum, the English subject not only assesses students' ability with regards to grammar, punctuation and spelling, reading and writing, but also evaluates their ability to communicate via spoken English.

THE IMPORTANCE OF SPOKEN ENGLISH

Pupils need to be taught how to:

- Verbally communicate to a high standard by conveying confidence, fluidity and personality.
- Improve their speaking by engaging with different word choices and language techniques.
- Participate in verbal debates, discussions and presentations.
- Demonstrate effective spoken English by improving speaking skills such as volume, tone, enthusiasm and interaction.

HOW TO IMPROVE YOUR SPEAKING SKILLS

Although there will not be a test about verbal communication, it is important that you are able to demonstrate great speaking skills, in order to enhance your learning and become a confident speaker.

On the following pages, we have provided a few TOP TIPS to help you improve your speaking skills.

Below is a diagram of all the key skills you should focus on in order to improve your speaking abilities.

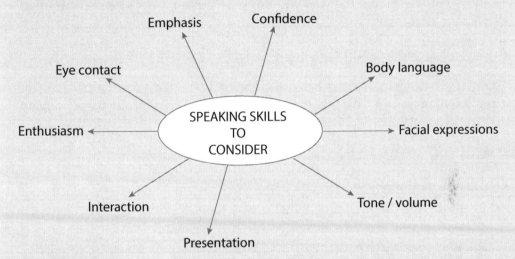

CONFIDENCE

Confidence is key in any situation that requires you to speak out loud. Particularly if you have to talk to a new or large group of people, it is important that you convey as much confidence as possible.

Confidence will not only show people that you know what you are talking about, but it makes the thought of public speaking a little less daunting.

How to improve your confidence:

- Practise! The more practice you undergo, the more confident you will become.
- Practise by yourself and with other people.
- Practise in front of a mirror.
- Understand that everyone makes mistakes. You're not expected to be perfect.
- Understand your strengths and weaknesses and work on those weaker areas.
- Ask for feedback and learn from what people tell you.
- Stay positive.

HOW TO IMPROVE YOUR SPOKEN ENGLISH

BODY LANGUAGE

The way you stand and the way you come across to the audience is another significant factor.

Body language will exert confidence.

Of course it depends on the type of situation you are in and the people you are presenting to. Are you presenting to a group of friends? Or are you giving a formal speech?

How to convey body language:

- Stand / sit upright.
- In a formal debate or presentation, you want to look as professional as possible.
- Avoid moving your arms too much. Place your hands down by your side.

FACIAL EXPRESSIONS

Your face needs to look engaging with both the content of your speech and the audience.

Some people have a very expressive face, and this helps them to convey meaning.

How to convey facial expressions:

- Use a mirror and practise your facial expressions.
- Create links between your content and your face. For example, if you are speaking about something serious and sad, you would want to avoid happy facial expressions.

HOW TO IMPROVE YOUR SPOKEN ENGLISH

TONE / VOLUME

The tone and volume of your voice plays a key factor in how you come across in verbal communication.

You need to understand how tone and volume of your voice can change the ambience of both the room and the content in which you are speaking.

How to improve tone and volume:

- Practise speaking at different volumes. If you are addressing a large audience, you will need to make sure that the people at the back of the room will be able to hear you.
- You want to avoid sounding monotonous. Just like singers have different tricks and tones with their singing voices, everyone's speaking voice can be changed so that they don't have just one tone.

PRESENTATION AND INTERACTION

This is one of the biggest things you will need to work on. Public speaking requires you to have great presentation skills.

When it comes to presentation, this includes everything:

- Body language
- Expressions
- Enthusiasm
- Interaction
- Eye contact

All of these make up your overall presentation skills.

The best way to practise presenting is to undergo lots of sample presentations. These don't have to be anything formal. Simply practise with a friend or family member – talk to them about a particular topic, and try to remember the aforementioned techniques.

HOW TO IMPROVE YOUR SPOKEN ENGLISH

ENTHUSIASM

In order to avoid sounding dull, you will want to make sure that you sound engaging. To do this, you will need to sound enthusiastic.

You can look and sound enthusiastic by drawing on all of the other speaking skills mentioned in this section.

EYE CONTACT

When speaking, it is considered polite to look people directly in the eye. However, this can be difficult if you are talking to a large number of people.

Effective eye contact:

- You need to avoid looking at the floor or quickly gazing around the room.
- If you're talking to one person, regularly make eye contact.
- If you're talking to a large group of people, try not to focus on just one person. Scan the room slowly. This will demonstrate that you are making an effort to make everyone feel included.

EMPHASIS

When speaking, a great technique to learn is to add emphasis in your speech.

This can be done in a number of ways:

- Add pauses for dramatic effect.
- If there is a certain word or phrase that you want to add more emphasis to, you can say it differently.
- You can emphasise certain words by using gestures.

You can practise adding emphasis to your speaking in order to become an effective speaker.

EXERCISES

EXERCISE 1

Stand in front of a mirror. Without speaking, look at how you present yourself. Remember, the key to good spoken English is presentation skills.

When looking in the mirror, focus on the following areas:

- Hand gestures
- Facial expressions
- Body posture
- Eye contact

Keep practising your presentation skills until you feel confident in your presenting skills. It is not only your language people will pay attention to, but the way you look.

EXERCISE 2

Why is eye contact important when addressing a group of people?

_____

_____

_____

_____

_____

_____

_____

_____

_____

EXERCISE 3

Below is The Queen's first speech in 1940. Read through her speech and then practise saying it out loud.

<u>As you did for the previous exercise, practise the following:</u>

- Hand gestures
- Facial expressions
- Tone of voice
- Body posture
- Eye contact

Begin by practising in front of a mirror. You could even attempt to video record yourself to see what your presentation skills look like. If you feel confident, try practising in front of friends and family.

THE QUEEEN'S SPEECH 1940

In wishing you all 'good evening' I feel that I am speaking to friends and companions who have shared with my sister and myself many a happy Children's Hour.

Thousands of you in this country have had to leave your homes and be separated from your fathers and mothers. My sister Margaret Rose and I feel so much for you as we know from experience what it means to be away from those we love most of all.

To you, living in new surroundings, we send a message of true sympathy and at the same time we would like to thank the kind people who have welcomed you to their homes in the country.

All of us children who are still at home think continually of our friends and relations who have gone overseas - who have travelled thousands of miles to find a wartime home and a kindly welcome in Canada, Australia, New Zealand, South Africa and the United States of America.

My sister and I feel we know quite a lot about these countries. Our father and mother have so often talked to us of their visits to different parts of the world. So it is not difficult for us to picture the sort of life you are all leading, and to think of all the new sights you must be seeing, and the adventures you must be having.

But I am sure that you, too, are often thinking of the Old Country. I know you won't forget us; it is just because we are not forgetting you that I want, on behalf of all the children at home, to send you our love and best wishes - to you and to your kind hosts as well.

Before I finish I can truthfully say to you all that we children at home are full of cheerfulness and courage. We are trying to do all we can to help our gallant sailors, soldiers and airmen, and we are trying, too, to bear our own share of the danger and sadness of war.

We know, every one of us, that in the end all will be well; for God will care for us and give us victory and peace. And when peace comes, remember it will be for us, the children of today, to make the world of tomorrow a better and happier place.

My sister is by my side and we are both going to say goodnight to you.

Come on, Margaret.

Goodnight, children.

Goodnight, and good luck to you all.

THE
REVISION
SERIES

SPEAKING ACTIVITIES AND GAMES

ACTIVITY 1

Find the informal words in the word search below.

Isn't	Dad	Alright	Cheers
Kinda	Booze	Gaff	Hiya
Dosh	Slammer	Wassup	Joint
Dunno	Innit	Nowt	Awesome

```
P  G  B  H  B  T  R  P  H  W  A  W  X  K  I  N  D  A
Y  D  S  R  Z  S  U  D  G  L  H  M  P  V  F  X  V  Q
M  O  H  G  U  S  U  Z  R  S  N  O  W  T  G  G  P  Y
O  S  M  C  S  N  Q  I  L  M  Z  U  W  V  H  X  M  I
B  R  B  A  N  X  G  O  U  U  G  Z  O  B  W  X  N  W
S  E  W  O  F  H  N  L  P  W  V  Q  R  Z  O  P  I  A
Y  E  X  E  T  M  X  P  S  H  M  D  O  I  R  O  U  E
G  H  D  X  K  Z  Q  P  Y  O  Q  U  I  B  I  A  Z  R
X  C  G  L  T  X  D  P  F  X  C  W  B  Q  M  I  V  E
Y  X  H  N  L  W  G  I  D  R  K  Q  K  O  Z  J  C  D
E  I  I  Y  W  G  I  A  J  M  T  Y  P  N  Q  J  D  K
M  M  O  N  M  U  I  L  F  B  M  K  O  Y  I  O  G  T
I  R  O  W  C  V  R  Q  Y  F  A  T  W  S  D  A  Q  Q
T  Z  Y  S  N  B  T  I  N  N  I  M  N  F  J  A  L  H
A  D  D  V  E  Q  S  O  L  O  E  R  R  S  O  Y  D  E
M  N  D  C  V  W  I  R  E  M  M  A  L  S  I  I  N  R
K  H  B  J  P  Z  A  H  Z  H  S  Y  N  I  N  H  R  F
V  N  G  D  Y  O  E  L  M  F  G  L  D  N  T  N  B  C
```

ACTIVITY 2

DEBATE TOPIC
Should homework be banned?

You are about to partake in a debate. The topic of this debate is: 'Should homework be banned?'

Using the table below, bullet point some arguments, both FOR and AGAINST.

After you have completed the table, start a debate with a friend or family member, and speak the points you have written. Remember, in debates, you need to be persuasive.

Consider the following when undergoing a debate:

- Pronunciation
- Language
- Body language
- Facial expressions
- Intentional pauses
- Expect interruptions

Remember, this exercise is to improve your speaking skills. This is a key learning curve for everyone, and is particularly important for students.

On the next page, you will find your debate table which you should fill in.

FOR	AGAINST

ACTIVITY 3

This is a role play exercise. You will need someone to help you practise your speaking skills.

For this exercise, imagine the following:

> You are a shop assistant in a shoe shop. A customer comes in. You notice that he is angry and storms to you, shouting and waving a box around.
>
> Your task is to create a role play.
>
> The opening line of your role play helper will be 'I am not satisfied with my purchase!'

This is a creative exercise that allows you to make up your own response. After the role play actor has said the line above, you need to continue the conversation and handle the situation.

<u>Focus on the following when responding to the actor:</u>

- Consider the language you should use. Remember, you are a shop assistant and therefore you need to remain professional.

- The role play actor could say anything, and therefore you need to be prepared to handle the situation.

- Consider your tone, actions and language.

Not only does this exercise improve your speaking skills, but it also allows you to improve your skills in dealing with pressurised and possibly confrontational situations. This will no doubt improve your confidence.

ACTIVITY 4

Write a speech addressing your classmates to vote for you to become head boy / head girl. Your speech should include valid reasons as to why you are the best candidate, and demonstrate how you plan to implement change and ideas, if you are appointed.

Within your speech, include the following:

- At least one rhetorical question;
- A pause for dramatic effect;
- Persuasive language;
- Involve your audience.

_____

_____

_____

_____

_____

_____

_____

_____

_____

_____

_____

_____

_____

Now practise your speech in front of a mirror or a person you know well. You should be aiming to look as natural and as confident as possible.

ACTIVITY 5

GAME

For this game, you will need 2+ players.

Below we have included 6 categories, each containing lots of words and/or phrases. You will take it in turns describing a word without using its name, which your fellow players must try to guess. The aim of this game is to improve your descriptive and on-the-spot speaking skills.

The rules of the game:

1. You will need to take it in turns to describe the word and/or phrase. You can either play by going round in a circle and letting the next person describe, or you can play by the person who guesses the word/phrase correctly to be the next person to describe.

2. For all of the words/phrases in this book, you will need to write them out on pieces of card (paper will work as well) and place them in a pack (just like a deck of cards).

3. You are not to mention the word/phrase written on the card. You are not to mention any key related words.

4. After you have used that card, place it at the bottom of the pile.

5. Even if you work through all of these cards, you can make up your own ones and add it to the pile.

Below are your six categories alongside all of the words/phrases that you can use for this game. The aim of this game is to improve your speaking skills and have some fun!

You have 30 seconds to try and describe the word/phrase on your card. If your time runs up, the next player will begin describing.

CATEGORY 1 = TOURIST ATTRACTIONS

London Eye	Eiffel Tower	Taj Mahal	Golden Gate Bridge
Statue of Liberty	Mount Everest	Grand Canyon	Central Park
Buckingham Palace	Great Wall of China	Notre Dame	Niagara Falls
Trevi Fountain	Sydney Opera House	Disneyland Park	Times Square
The Shard	Stonehenge	London Zoo	Leeds Castle

CATEGORY 2 = FAMOUS PEOPLE

David Beckham	The Queen	Barack Obama	Kim Kardashian
Robbie Williams	George Clooney	Marilyn Monroe	Harry Styles
Steven Spielberg	Kate Middleton	Leonardo DiCaprio	Charles Dickens
William Shakespeare	Abraham Lincoln	Jamie Oliver	Lord Alan Sugar
Henry VIII	Winston Churchill	Brad Pitt	Kate Winslet

CATEGORY 3 = COUNTRIES

Australia	China	France	New Zealand
Thailand	Portugal	Germany	Malta
Kenya	India	Italy	Cyprus
Czech Republic	Brazil	Argentina	Finland
Hong Kong	Ireland	Spain	Madagascar

CATEGORY 4 = OBJECTS

Waterfall	Fireplace	Mobile phone	Carpet
Tyre	Fan	Stickers	Stamps
Games Console	Advert	Trophy	Vase
Bean bag	Printer	Violin	Plaster
Fishing net	Compass	Tea bag	Speakers

CATEGORY 5 = ANIMALS

Penguin	Polar Bear	Komodo Dragon	Giraffe
Ant	Stingray	Panda	Alligator
Eagle	Seal	Ostrich	Turtle
Cobra	Zebra	Skunk	Octopus
Jellyfish	Wolf	Crocodile	Hedgehog

CATEGORY 6 = SPORTS AND STARS

Archery	Sailing	Hockey	Lewis Hamilton
Usain Bolt	Tiger Woods	Ice Skating	Gymnastics
Football	Bobsledding	Lionel Messi	Cristiano Ronaldo
Michael Jordan	Ice Hockey	Serena Williams	Tennis
Squash	Netball	Swimming	Snooker

ACTIVITY 6

For this exercise, we will focus on your pronunciation.

The words listed below are some of the most common words that people struggle to pronounce correctly.

For each word, read how the word should be pronounced and then say it out loud. Say it 3 or 4 times to ensure you pronounce the word correctly.

a) Phenomenon

   (Fi – nom – uh – non)

b) Anonymous

   (Uh – non – uh – mus)

c) Sandwiches

   (Sand – witch – es)

d) Mischievous

   (Mis – che – vous)

e) Millennium

   (Me – len – e – erm)

f) Colonel

   (Ker – nal)

g) Anemone

   (Uh – nem – uh – nee)

ACTIVITY 7

TONGUE TWISTERS

Read the tongue twisters and practise saying them out loud.

1

She sells sea shells on the sea shore.

2

Red lorry, yellow lorry, red lorry, yellow lorry...

3

Baboon, bamboo, baboon, bamboo, baboon, bamboo...

4

How much wood would a woodchuck chuck

If a woodchuck could chuck wood?

He would chuck, he would, as much as he could,

And chuck as much wood as a woodchuck would

If a woodchuck could chuck wood.

Why not come up with your own and get your friends and family to read them?

ACTIVITY 8

Here is another role play exercise.

This role play will be based on William Shakespeare's play, *As You Like It.*

For each character in the play, write down a few notes about the way in which the character should be acted.

Focus on the following:

- How will they act?
- What characteristics do they have?
- What language is used?
- Consider your pronunciation.

This is a great exercise to not only get you speaking in a role of someone else, but it also provides some understanding of how language in Shakespeare's work differs from our own.

When you've finished practising your role, act it out in front of people. You can get as creative as you want. Try acting out the character in different ways. If you're feeling really adventurous, you may want to try acting out the character by changing the language to our everyday language.

Once you've played one character, swap around and play the other character.

ORLANDO

ADAM

ORLANDO

Why, whither, Adam, wouldst thou have me go?

ADAM

No matter whither, so you come not here.

ORLANDO

What, wouldst thou have me go and beg my food?
Or with a base and boisterous sword enforce
A thievish living on the common road?
This I must do, or know not what to do:
Yet this I will not do, do how I can;
I rather will subject me to the malice
Of a diverted blood and bloody brother.

ADAM

But do not so. I have five hundred crowns,
The thrifty hire I saved under you father,
Which I did store to be my foster-nurse
When service should in my old limbs lie lame
And unregarded age in corners thrown:
Take that, and He that doth the ravens feed,
Yea, providently caters for the sparrow,
Be comfort to my age! Here is the gold;
And all this I give you. Let me be your servant:
Though I look old, yet I am strong and lusty;
For in my youth I never did apply
Hot and rebellious liquors in my blood,
Nor did not with unbashful forehead woo
The means of weakness and debility;
Therefore my age is as a lusty winter,
Frosty, but kindly: let me go with you;

I'll do the service of a younger man
In all your business and necessities.

ORLANDO

O good old man, how well in thee appears
The constant service of the antique world,
When service sweat for duty, not for meed!
Thou art not for the fashion of these times,
Where none will sweat but for promotion,
And having that, do choke their service up
Even with the having: it is not so with thee.
But, poor old man, thou prunest a rotten tree,
That cannot so much as a blossom yield
In lieu of all thy pains and husbandry.
But come thy ways: we'll go along together,
And ere we have thy youthful wages spent,
We'll light upon some settled low content.

ADAM

Master, go on, and I will follow thee,
To the last gasp, with truth and loyalty.
From seventeen years till now almost fourscore
Here lived I, but now live here no more.
At seventeen years many their fortunes seek;
But as fourscore it is too late a week:
Yet fortune cannot recompense me better
Than to die well and not my master's debtor.
   Exit.

ACTIVITY 9

GAME

To play this game, you need:

1. A stopwatch;
2. Topics/subjects written on individual pieces of paper;
3. 4 or more people.

How to play:

1. Cut up a load of different topics and put them in a bowl/container.
2. One person will call on someone to play first. That person will have to pick a piece of paper out from the container.
3. That person will then give the piece of the paper to the caller who will then say "You have one minute to talk about [enter subject topic here]."
4. The aim of the game is to talk for that whole minute. Award 10 points for speaking the whole minute, 8 points for speaking 45 seconds, 6 points for 30 seconds, 4 points for 20 seconds and 2 points for 10 seconds. Anything less than 10 seconds, you should award just 1 point.
5. Keep tally of the score.
6. Take it in turns being the caller. Let everyone have a turn.

Some ideas for topics:

Animated Films	Shakespeare	London	Flowers	Poems
Pop stars	Movies	Books	History	Cars
Rivers	Directors	Musicals	Desserts	Music

ACTIVITY 10

Below is a scene from William Shakespeare's play, *Othello*. This exercise can be undertaken by just yourself, or with another person.

<u>As you did for the previous exercise, practise the following:</u>

- Hand gestures
- Facial expressions
- Tone of voice
- Body posture
- Eye contact

Begin by practising in front of a mirror. You could even attempt to video record yourself to see what your presentation skills look like. If you feel confident, try practising in front of friends and family.

OTHELLO

This fellow's of exceeding honesty
And knows all qualities, with a learned spirit,
Of human dealings. If I do prove her haggard,
Though that her jesses were my dear heart-strings,
I'd whistle her off and let her down the wind
To prey at fortune. Haply for I am black,
And have not those soft parts of conversation
That chamberers have, or for I am declined
Into the vale of years – yet that's not much –
She's gone, I am abused, and my relief
Must be to loathe her. O curse of marriage,
That we can call these delicate creatures ours
And not their appetites! I had rather be a toad
And live upon the vapour of a dungeon
Than keep a corner in the thing I love

For others' uses. Yet 'tis the plague of great one,
Prerogativ'd are they less than the base;
'Tis destiny unshunnable, like death:
Even then this forked plague is fated to us
When we do quicken. Look where she comes.
   Enter Desdemona and Emilia
If she be false, O then heaven mocks itself!
I'll not believe't.

DESDEMONA
How now, my dear Othello?
Your dinner, and the generous islanders
By you invited, do attend your presence.

OTHELLO
I am to blame.

DESDEMONA
Why do you speak so faintly?
Are you not well?

OTHELLO
I have a pain upon my forehead here.

DESDEMONA
Faith, that's with watching; 'twill away again.
Let me but bind it hard, within this hour
It will be well.

OTHELLO
Your napkin is too little.
   He puts the handkerchief from him, and drops it
Let it alone. Come, I'll go in with you.

DESDEMONA
I am very sorry that you are not well.
                       [Exeunt Othello and Desdemona]

ACTIVITY 11

WHO AM I?

For this game, you will require 2 or more people. The idea of this game is to guess who you are by asking 'yes' or 'no' questions.

How to play:

1. On a sticky note, or a blank piece of paper, write down the name of a famous person. This can be anyone.

2. The aim of the game is to guess what name is written on the piece of paper.

3. If you use sticky notes, stick it to the other person's forehead. If you use a blank piece of paper, get some cellotape and stick it to the their backs, so that they can't see it.

4. You will each take it in turns asking questions. For example: 'Am I a boy?' 'Am I a singer?' 'Am I English?' etc.

5. Whoever guesses the name first, wins!

This game is great for interacting with other people. Not only is it a fun game to play, but it will also improve your cognitive skills, as well as your speaking skills.

ACTIVITY 12

BACK TO BACK

This game requires 2 people. The idea of this game is to guess what word or phrase the other person is speaking, by drawing what you think it is.

How to play:

1. Begin by sitting back to back.

2. One of you will be the drawer and the other person will be the speaker.

3. The speaker will think of a word or phrase and write it down on a piece of paper in front of them.

4. The speaker will then describe what it is, without actually mentioning it!

5. From the description, the drawer will have to draw what is being described.

6. At the end of the drawing, the drawer must then guess what it is that they have drawn, if they guess it correctly, then win a point. If they get it wrong, the speaker gets a point.

7. Take it in turns being the speaker and drawer.

This game not only enhances spoken English, but it also improve other key skills such as visualisation and creative thinking.

ACTIVITY 13

TELL A STORY

This game requires 2 or more people. This game is great to get to know someone while improving writing and speaking skills.

How to play:

1. One person should come up with a topic which can be relatable to everyone. For example:

   a. What is your biggest fear?

   b. What is your favourite place?

   c. What is your ideal holiday?

   d. Who is your inspiration?

2. Everyone will then need to write a story based on their personal experience. This is a great way to get to know new people.

3. Then, you will each place your stories in a pile, face down.

4. One person can then shuffle them, and hand them out at random.

5. You will each take it in turns to read out the story you have been given.

6. Once you have read the story, the person who's story it is can come forward (or not).

7. If that person would like to share their story, the rest of the group can then ask follow-up questions. If the person wishes to remain anonymous, then you will move on to the next person, and read out the next story.

This is a great way to not only work on written communication, but also read and express feelings and experiences based on somebody else.

ACTIVITY 14

MAKE A VIDEO

To make a video, you can either work on your own or make it with a friend or family member.

<u>What to do:</u>

1. Have someone give you a topic. For example:

   a. Walking home from school

   b. What you get up to at the weekend

   c. Going to a party

   d. How to behave at a friend's house

2. The video should capture the key things about the topic you are talking about. Remember this video not only should show your surroundings, but it should also film yourself talking to the camera (or potentially whoever will watch this i.e. a teacher, friend, family, etc.).

3. Remember that the idea of this video is to demonstrate your speaking skills. You want to be as descriptive as possible. You want to engage your make-believe audience.

This is a great way to combine technology with spoken English. This is a quick and easy method to practise your speaking skills. You can do this as many times as you want. Simply use your phone or your tablet and get recording!

ACTIVITY 15

SPOKEN BINGO

Are you ready for a game of bingo?

This game will require 4 or more people. Similar to the normal bingo game, you will need to cross off words on your bingo card, until you have none left, and then you shout out 'bingo'.

How to play:

1. Prepare blank bingo cards. I have provided an example on the following page.

2. Have someone (a teacher or parent) come up with a list of 50 words. These words could be on a particular topic, or completely random.

3. These words need to be shown to everyone.

4. Then, each person will then choose 25 words they want to use to fill in their bingo card.

5. The 50 words should be cut up and placed in a pot or hat. Each person will take it in turns going up to the front, picking a word at random and describing that word. They are not to say what the word is. They have 3 sentences to describe the word.

6. That person will sit back down. If a person has that word, they can cross it off. If they don't, they won't cross it off.

7. Continue describing words until a person gets all of the words. That person would then have to shout 'bingo'. Have the teacher or parent check that all the words have been correctly crossed off.

8. You can always spice things up and play for 1 line, 2 lines and a full house.

SAMPLE BINGO CARD TEMPLATE

NEED A LITTLE EXTRA HELP WITH KEY STAGE 3 (KS3) ENGLISH?

How2Become have created other FANTASTIC guides to help you and your child prepare for Key Stage Three (KS3) English.

These exciting guides are filled with fun and interesting facts for your child to engage with to ensure that their revision is fun, and their learning is improved! Invest in your child's future today!

FOR MORE INFORMATION ON OUR KEY STAGE 3 (KS3) GUIDES, PLEASE CHECK OUT THE FOLLOWING:

WWW.HOW2BECOME.COM

Get Access To

FREE

Psychometric
Tests

www.PsychometricTestsOnline.co.uk